To

_____

From

_____

Date

_____

THE LIFE & TIMES OF
A CAT LOVER

PHOTOGRAPHS BY
BEV SPARKS

HARVEST HOUSE PUBLISHERS

EUGENE, OREGON

THE LIFE AND TIMES OF A CAT LOVER

Text Copyright © 2009 by Harvest House Publishers

Artwork Copyright © by Bev Sparks by arrangement with The Greeting Place

Text written and compiled by Hope Lyda

Published by Harvest House Publishers

Eugene, Oregon 97402

www.harvesthousepublishers.com

ISBN 978-0-7369-2604-1

Design and production by Koechel Peterson & Associates, Inc., Minneapolis, Minnesota

Harvest House Publishers has made every effort to trace the ownership of all poems and quotes. In the event of a question arising from the use of a poem or quote, we regret any error made and will be pleased to make the necessary correction in future editions of this book.

Printed in China

09 10 11 12 13 14 15 / LP / 10 9 8 7 6 5 4 3 2 1

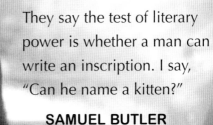

They say the test of literary power is whether a man can write an inscription. I say, "Can he name a kitten?"

SAMUEL BUTLER

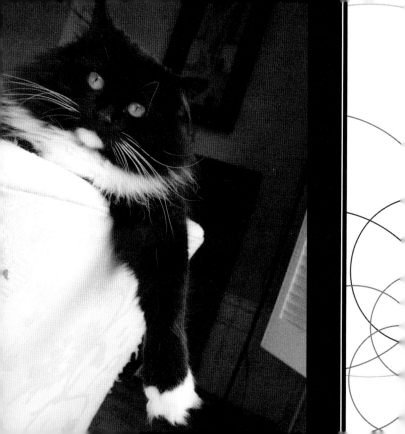

THE REALLY GREAT THING about cats is their endless variety. One can pick a cat to fit almost any kind of décor, color, income, personality, or mood. But under the fur, whatever color it may be, there still lies, essentially unchanged, one of the world's free souls.

ERIC GURNEY

Cats don't like change without their consent.

ROGER A. CARAS

CAT LOVERS' CORNER

THE MAN who has made "Yo, Dawg!" a popular phrase among *American Idol* fans has a soft spot for felines, it seems. Randy Jackson put his celebrity power behind Morris' Million Cat Rescue sponsored by 9Lives. Their noble goal? To get one million homeless cats adopted. The singer, songwriter, musician, and producer put his kitty kibble where it counts—he adopted a cat from the program and, of course, named it Dawg. Infamous Morris the Cat is the official "spokesperson" for the big charitable undertaking.

Most cats, when they are Out,
want to be In, and vice versa,
and often simultaneously.

LOUIS CAMUTI

Perhaps it is because cats do not live by
human patterns, do not fit themselves
into prescribed behavior, that they are so
united to creative people.

ANDRE NORTON

WHY WE LOVE OUR CATS

STEALTH. Cats maneuver under the radar of human perception. They materialize in the kitchen when they smell something enticing being cooked. They appear out of nowhere to perch on us so they can look down at us while we are sleeping at 5:00 in the morning. Their fur appears on furniture or in the car where we swear they've never, ever been. They emerge from a secret napping location in the bedroom after we've called for them outdoors until our voices are hoarse. But their greatest trick is that they quietly but confidently sneak their way into our hearts...and take up residence forever.

As every cat owner knows,
nobody owns a cat.

ELLEN PERRY BERKELEY

Since each of us is blessed with only one life, why not live it with a cat?

ROBERT STEARNS

Alexander the Great, Napoleon, and Hitler…
were apparently terrified of small felines…If you
want to conquer the world, you had better not
share even a moment with an animal that refuses
to be conquered at any price, by anyone.

DESMOND MORRIS

IT IS SAID that Charles Lindbergh didn't take his kitten, Patsy, when he flew across the Atlantic in 1927 because he didn't want to put her at risk. That's love.

THE CAT went here and there
And the moon spun round like a top,
And the nearest kin of the moon,
The creeping cat, looked up.
Black Minnaloushe stared at the moon,
For, wander and wail as he would,
The pure cold light in the sky
Troubled his animal blood.
Minnaloushe runs in the grass
Lifting his delicate feet,
Do you dance, Minnaloushe,
do you dance?

WILLIAM BUTLER YEATS

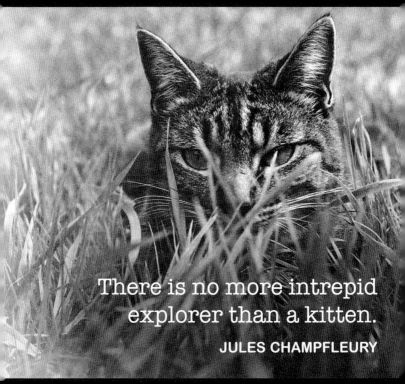

There is no more intrepid
explorer than a kitten.

JULES CHAMPFLEURY

WHY WE LOVE OUR CATS

BEFORE THEY ARE our landlords, our masters, the keepers of our affection...cats start out as tumbling, lanky, funny kittens who chase their tails and spin out in the hallway after being chased by imaginary foes. Their energy is infectious. For such small beings, they have the courage of their large cat relatives in the jungles. Haven't we all witnessed a blob of a kitten attack a large chaise or the pant leg of a six-foot-tall human? When we get staid and boring and timid, kittens inspire laughter, whimsy, and bravado. They extend an open invitation to a perpetual playdate. Are you ready to let loose? Discover your equivalent to a ball of yarn (which might just happen to be a ball of yarn!) and join the fun.

You can keep a dog; but it is the cat who keeps people, because cats find humans useful domestic animals.

GEORGE MIKES

You call to a dog, and a dog will break its neck to get to you. Dogs just want to please. Call to a cat, and its attitude is, "What's in it for me?"

LEWIS GRIZZARD

CAT LOVERS and literature lovers might have the same location at the top of their "places to see" list. The Ernest Hemingway Home and Museum in Key West, Florida, is also home to a colony of more than 60 cats. About half of these cats are polydactyl (extra toes), and it is believed that many are descendants of a six-toed cat Hemingway received from a ship's captain.

No matter how much cats
fight, there always seems
to be plenty of kittens.

ABRAHAM LINCOLN

When I play with my cat,

who knows but that she regards me

more as a plaything than I do her?

MICHEL DE MONTAIGNE

WHY WE LOVE OUR CATS

IN THE MOVIES, it is the watchdog who gets all of the attention and accolades. There's often a scene in which a lean, strong Doberman chases away the bad guy and saves the humans. But the attentive watchcat who perches in the window or under a shrub for hours and observes every move of every squirrel, pedestrian, shadow, or leaf rarely gets due credit. Her patience is worthy of praise. Her keen ability to zoom in on movement deserves kudos. And when she stands with muscles taut, waiting for the perfect moment to pounce, she is a statue-worthy image. Let's hear it for the plump house cat, the willowy youngster, and the sly and stocky tomcat. They might not steal the scene, but they sure do take it in.

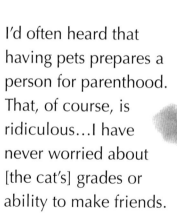

I'd often heard that having pets prepares a person for parenthood. That, of course, is ridiculous...I have never worried about [the cat's] grades or ability to make friends.

MARGE KENNEDY

Cleanliness in the
cat world is usually
a virtue put above
godliness.

CARL VAN VECHTEN

CAT LOVERS' CORNER

THROUGH THE DECADES the White House has often been a residence for intelligent, courageous, notable, and noble creatures known as the cat. Here are some of the presidents who let a cat in the house during their watch and if known, the name of the cat who was in charge.

George W. Bush	India
Bill Clinton	Socks
Jimmy Carter	Misty Malarky Ying Yang (Amy Carter's Siamese cat)
Gerald Ford	Shan (Susan Ford's Siamese cat)
John F. Kennedy	Tom Kitten
Calvin Coolidge	Tiger and Blacky
Theodore Roosevelt	Tom Quartz and Slippers
Rutherford Hayes	Owned the first Siamese kitten to reach America and other kittens
Abraham Lincoln	Tabby

Any glimpse into
the life of an
animal quickens
our own and
makes it so much
the larger and
better in every way.

JOHN MUIR

By associating with the cat,
one only risks becoming richer.

COLETTE

WE KEEP TRACK OF promises, duties, distractions, and responsibilities. But we forget to sit and be still. Or worse...we forget *how* to be still. Cats become our teachers in the way of lounging. They stretch, yawn, and then let their weight sink into the couch cushions. Cats are heat-seeking devices who search for the coziest patch of sun on the floor and then lie there, still and satisfied. Other times they jump up beside us and lean against us. And while they seek their own comfort and warmth, they give us those very same essentials. When a purring, lovely mass of fur is slumbering on our laps, those once-urgent distractions don't seem so tempting. And for a moment, we let the weight of our lives sink into the couch cushion...and we are still.

A charm of cats is that they seem to live in a world of their own, just as much as if it were a real dimension of space.

**HARRIET
PRESCOTT
SPOFFORD**

CAT LOVERS' CORNER

AUTHOR AND ARTIST Edward Lear created the classic rhyme "The Owl and the Pussycat" and was likely inspired by his tabby, Foss. He cared about Foss so much that when he had to move to Italy, he asked that his new house be designed just like his home in England so that Foss could more easily adapt.

A cat is there when you call her—if she doesn't have anything better to do.

BILL ADLER

Do our cats name us? My former husband swore that Humphrey and Dolly and Bean Blossom called me The Big Hamburger.

ELEANORA WALKER

PURR. PURR. PURR. It's the most wonderful sound. Whether our cat is lying in the crook of our arm as the sun rises or is curled up on a stack of papers beside our computer while we work, his purr calms our nerves. Cats communicate their contentment with the moment and in the moment. Their purr proclaims their warm affection and a certain level of security with the people in their presence. When we are stubborn to express our happiness or are unable to recognize the contentment in a moment, we miss out on entrusting and sharing our joy with those around us.

Cats also purr when they are afraid or need to soothe themselves. We, however, tend to look for ways to ignore our feelings and suppress our need to be comforted.

The purr is a simple yet amazing way that our cats reach across the divide between their language and our own. Be thankful for the gift of daily blessings including your cat's good vibrations and the pleasure he purrs into your life.

In a cat's eye, all things belong to cats.

ENGLISH PROVERB

Cats are absolute
individuals, with
their own ideas about
everything, including the
people they own.

JOHN DINGMAN

CAT LOVERS' CORNER

ACTRESS TIPPI HEDREN is not only known for her role in *The Birds*...but is known for her role in saving cats. Hedren became passionate about the graceful, powerful large cats of Africa. She founded the nonprofit Roar Foundation and Shambala Preserve, which houses African lions, leopards, Siberian and Bengal tigers, mountain lions, and other exotic animals. The philanthropic actress now lives by Shambala on the edge of the Mojave Desert and even leads tours of the amazing 80-acre habitat.

He lies there, purring and dreaming, shifting his limbs now and then in an ecstasy of cushioned comfort. He seems the incarnation of everything soft and silky and velvety, without a sharp edge in his composition, a dreamer whose philosophy is sleep and let sleep.

H.H. MUNRO

Time spent with cats
is never wasted.

COLETTE

CAT LOVERS' CORNER

IN 1942, Anne Frank and her family went into hiding to escape Nazi persecution. She mentions her beloved cat, Moortje, numerous times. In the following quote, she references the day they went into hiding and she had to leave her cat behind. "At seven-thirty we too closed the door behind us; Moortje, my cat, was the only living creature I said good-bye to. According to a note we left for Mr. Gouldschmidt, she was to be taken to the neighbours, who would give her a good home."

Nearly two years later she wrote in her diary, "I can also understand my homesickness and yearning for Moortje. The whole time I've been here I've longed unconsciously and at times consciously for trust, love, and physical affection. This longing may change in intensity, but it's always there."

Cats know how to obtain
food without labor, shelter
without confinement, and
love without penalties.

W.L. GEORGE

Cats are a mysterious kind of folk.

There is more passing in their minds

than we are aware of.

SIR WALTER SCOTT

Kitty Treats

CAT LOVERS' CORNER

A "MARMALADE" or ginger tabby cat named Jock was Sir Winston Churchill's sidekick. Jock slept in Churchill's bed, dined at his table, and attended Cabinet meetings. Churchill even commissioned a painting of his beloved Jock.

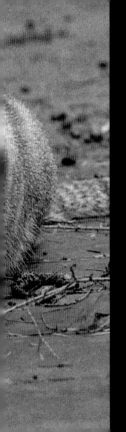

Dogs come when they're called; cats take a message and get back to you.

MARY BLY

There's no need for a piece of sculpture in a home that has a cat.

WESLEY BATES

Mice amused him, but he usually considered them too small game to be taken seriously; I have seen him play for an hour with a mouse and then let him go with a royal condescension.

CHARLES DUDLEY WARNER

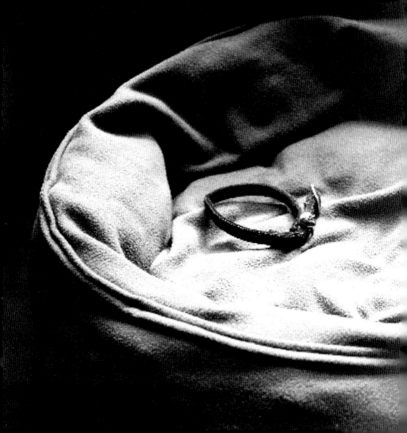

Of all God's creatures, there is only one that cannot be made slave of the leash. That one is the cat. If man could be crossed with the cat, it would improve the man, but it would deteriorate the cat.

MARK TWAIN

Of all animals, he alone attains
to the Contemplative Life.

ANDREW LANG

I love cats because I love my
home and after a while they
become its visible soul.

JEAN COCTEAU

Cats seem to go on the principle that it never does
any harm to ask for what you want.

JOSEPH WOOD KRUTCH

God made the cat in order to give man the pleasure of caressing the tiger.

AUTHOR UNKNOWN